BEYOND CALLING DISTANCE

Esther Morgan was born in 1970 in Kidderminster, Worcestershire. After reading English at Newnham College, Cambridge, she worked as a volunteer at the Wordsworth Trust in Grasmere, Cumbria. She took an MA in Creative Writing at the University of East Anglia in 1996-97 and has since taught part-time on the undergraduate creative writing programme at UEA. In 1998 she took part in the Creative Connections exchange programme between Britain and Australia, teaching at Edith Cowan University in Perth. She edits the annual UEA new poetry anthology *Reactions* (EAS/Pen&inc.).

Her poems have appeared in many magazines. She won an Eric Gregory Award for her poetry in 1998, and in 1999 she received an Eastern Arts writer's bursary. *Beyond Calling Distance* (Bloodaxe Books, 2001) is her first book of poems.

Esther Morgan

BEYOND CALLING DISTANCE

BLOODAXE BOOKS

ISBN: 1 85224 570 0

First published 2001 by
Bloodaxe Books Ltd,
Highgreen,
Tarset,
Northumberland NE48 1RP.

Bloodaxe Books Ltd acknowledges
the financial assistance of Northern Arts.

Cover printing by J. Thomson Colour Printers Ltd, Glasgow.

Printed in Great Britain by
Cromwell Press Ltd, Trowbridge, Wiltshire.

for my parents

Acknowledgements

Acknowledgements are due to the editors of the following publications in which some of these poems first appeared: *Acumen, First Pressings* (Faber & Faber, 1998), *New Writing* (Picador/British Council, 2001), *Raw Edge, Stand, The Rialto* and *Westerly* (Australia).

'Other Halves' won the New Forest Poetry Competition in 1998. Several of the poems were broadcast on *Poetica* (ABC Australia).

I would like to thank the Society of Authors and their judges for an Eric Gregory Award in 1998, and East England Arts for a writer's bursary in 1999.

In addition I would like to thank the many people who have helped me with this collection for their support, advice and inspiration: Sally-Ann and Paul Armitage, Gerard Benson, Bridget Gardner, Anna Garry, Matthew Hollis, Douglas Kyle, Graham Mort, Andrew Motion, Andrew Northern, Helen Oswald, George Szirtes, Hugo Williams, Morgan Yasbincek, Miranda Yates. Thank you Kelvyn for being there.

Contents

The Sea

One night the tide went out
and never came back in –
its shoals of moonlight lost
beyond our horizon.

We woke to a desert
a salt-crusted silence.
For weeks the churches were full.
Then they were empty.

The sea became a myth
our thin children don't believe in.
They mock our obsolete knowledge
of trade winds and currents.

They turn their backs on the docks
where the boats are all sinking,
white masts leaning at angles
like a forest of dying birches.

We grow long-sighted
watching for sails
in the shimmering heat.
We fall asleep

listening to shells.

Fifth of November

I draw the curtains, turn the TV up.
The dog's already cringing, despite a shot
to calm her down. She trembles

like the fringing on a lampshade
as a distant earthquake starts.
Hair-trigger hearing; she barks

as the postman changes gear
a mile from home, cocks her head
at the silence before the phone rings.

She senses storms hours in advance,
cowering as the wind roars and flattens
fields of corn in the distant Borders.

Now her ears, fine-tuned into the dark,
are flickering, picking up the spurt
of each struck match, the sizzle of fuses.

She creeps into my lap, her tremor
thrilling through my ribs. I croon
It's all right, but she's deaf

to comforting. Her eyes slide sideways
showing their whites. I see clouds
scarfing the moon like gun smoke,

a crowd of pale faces lifted to the sky,
children covering their ears
ready to scream.

Under the Bridge
31 December, 1996

Something fells him
full-length across the ice.
He stares all night into the mud,
his back to the stars,
pulse counting down.

Midnight.
Rockets explode.
All over the world
police link arms
for *Auld Lang Syne*.

In the foggy dawn
he's lifted, dummy-stiff,
hands-up in his Christmas gloves.
His blood's ebbed warmth
has thawed his imprint

in the snow. Cars crawl home.
In empty pubs
balloons are shrivelling
to the ground.
The evidence melts.

Water starts flowing.

Double Glazed

The advert impressed them –
a white feather
floating to the floor
while a helicopter
thrashed the garden.

A glass door slides –
their lives are guillotined.
He watches her
circling rooms
like a goldfish.

She watches him,
his silent whistling
as he digs the beds.
They try to read
each other's lips.

Tonight, curtains drawn,
TV loud with gunfire,
they are proof against
whatever it is
that slams out of the storm.

He discovers it next morning,
holds it up like a hunter
for a photograph –
stiff as stone,
its wings still spread.

Detecting

Metal is only the medium
you choose to speak through –
its dolphin song of clicks and whistles
telling me I'm getting warmer
as I search the deserted beach.

I save everything you give me –
empty cans, silver sweet wrappers,
the loose change lost by families.
In moonlight my room shines
like a reliquary. You slipped

out of life so easily,
shedding your dress like a skin,
veiling yourself in the waves'
crewel-work of lace.
I've no kept bone to kiss,

just this watch I found one night,
its face still luminous,
buried in the low-tide sand.
It isn't yours – the steel bracelet
too slack for such slightness

but holding its stainless links
while I drift asleep,
my fingers dream your wrist,
can almost feel a pulse tick
beneath the salt-stopped hands.

The Ring Man

They say he could sense gold
hidden in the sand – an ache
at the root of his divining tongue
told his hands where to dig.

They say a fortune of rings
bit deep into his sea-stained skin,
that his thick knuckles were dusted
with the sparkle of lost stones.

My mother swears she never saw him
without his hands thrust in his pockets,
but I've heard the women of the town
smuggled their hearts down to the harbour

where they whispered to dark sailors
and their naked fingers danced.
And there's a rumour he was buried
with his wrist stumps dipped in tar,

that our fathers wrecked themselves
on the look-out for likenesses
in the faces of their sleeping sons.
Now in certain lights

stealing glimpses of myself
I see a stranger in my eyes'
horizons, a Russian tsarina
in the slant of my cheekbones.

But a question could change forever
the weather in a home,
lives bruising into storm.
We are all wedded to silence.

The Reason

It's because you never left
these endless fields

where an oak tree sails the horizon
like a lost galleon

where rabbits crouch in mad-dog heat
under a sky full of eyes

where a gunshot scatters acres of birds
leaving wires like empty staves

where a road runs straight for hours
towards a shimmering spire

where a man can live all his life
beyond calling distance.

The Cows

They appeared in summer, huge shoulders
shambling through the gloom,
pushing through air like green water.

Their patience drew me, the way
they only flicked their ears, submitted to
the bluebottles that glittered their eyes,

or their passive resistance to rain,
huddled in the lea of the hawthorn,
water coursing their mountainous flanks.

My mother thought them dangerous,
their hooves churning the field to mud.
She warned me to keep the barbed fence between

us, but I always slipped through
to stand like a priest or sacrifice
in the midst of their steaming henge.

They seemed to dream as they chewed the cud,
working their cool alchemy, earth into
cream, dung as rich as cake mixture.

I knew in Africa nomads tapped their throats for blood,
in India they wandered sacred, untouched,
measuring the dust between villages.

I made them offerings –
handfuls of grass proffered shyly,
honoured if they slubbered my palms clean.

The tags in their ears made them gypsyish
and I longed to follow them,
their slow hypnosis under the moon

stealing me through the meadow
and into the mist that made
ghost ships of the silver birches.

But they only shifted their weight in the mud,
garlanded by the evening sun,
oblivious under their haloes of flies.

The first warm morning

I move through the house
opening windows stiff as joints
after months of rain.

Curtains lacy with sunlight
gesture into an empty room.
Sounds enter on the air:

an occasional car passing,
the clink of tools renovating,
a playground's archive of laughter.

Last Summer

She spent that summer cycling up and down
the long, straight private drive,
skidding to a halt
each time she reached the road.

With both hands on the handlebars
and one foot on the ground
she stared across the open fields
listening –

the pine trees creaked like masts,
voices hummed through telegraph wires,
cows lay silent in the shade
settled heavily in the long grass.

All summer she listened to the heat-stilled world,
her thumb resting on the rusted bell,
the front wheel turned back towards home
like a broken neck.

Pressure

She can sense it,
sickening like seaweed for storm;

migraine weather
darkening the rooms,

an atmosphere inside the house,
close and sticky

like a hot hand
clamped over the mouth.

Sent to bed early
she sweats it out,

her thoughts hatching
like flying ants

as she lies there waiting
for her mother to break.

Spirits

They infest the silence
    behind doors
hide between
    layers of wallpaper
under the hush
  of thick carpets.

They live in the glint
    of cut glass
in the print of lips
    at the edge
in the needle's hiss
    before the blues.

They haunt her mother
    through lost afternoons
slip between clock ticks.
    They are present as breath
dancing on the tip
    of her peppermint tongue.

Self Portrait

She is drawing and redrawing herself,
her skin sore from erasure.

She tries again and again for a likeness
to somebody real.

Instead she is layering ghosts:
eyes behind eyes behind eyes

mouths behind mouths behind mouths
all of them closed.

Images on Glass

She makes herself up –
thick war paint for a brave,
but there's a line on her neck
where white skin begins.
She shivers in the night-club queue,

gives her false age like a question.
Inside, the girls are Vidal
flicking silky blonde sheets,
the boys take a butchers
at the dance floor meat.

She acts animated –
cartoon sexy in crushed velvet
pouting snakebite from a plastic glass.
A boy interrogates –
she can't hear but fakes

a smile, says yes
to everything, hoping
that's the right answer.
He drags her off into the corner
for a concrete-mixer snog.

Girls clip-clop to the bogs in pairs
like freak ark animals. She's sick
as quietly as possible,
comes out smiling with sore lips,
sticks some more slap on.

The music beats against her heart,
a mirror ball splits her
into infinity, a stranger's arms
hold her together for the last slow dance –
you were wonderful tonight.

The lights come up on a reflection
she can't recognise – black eyes,
a smeared red mouth. She creeps back
home like a thief. In the dark
she takes off her face.

Office Angel

She migrates across the dusty city
on invisible wings,

a quiet presence moving
through empty summer offices,

watering silk flowers,
answering calls for girls

gone away to the coast.
Lunch hours she loses herself

in a maze of bleached streets,
stands in a square of heat

scattering crumbs
for the crippled pigeons.

Through long afternoons
the thick crêpe blinds

bandage the light,
an exit sign flickers

like a tired green eye.
Inside her headache

a voice dictates, her fingers
slip, translating messages

into unknown tongues.
At the end of the day

she leaves her desk
like the Marie Celeste.

As she gives in her identity
pass and steps through glass

into sun, it's as if
she never existed.

The Lost Word

She's lost a word
and searches for it everywhere –
behind the sofa, at the back
of dusty cupboards and drawers.
She picks through the buzzing rubbish sacks.

Under the carpet she finds lots of others
she'd forgotten she'd swept there,
but not the one she's looking for.
The trouble is it's small – only two letters –
though no less valuable for that.

She stands racking her brains
for the last time she used it
but all that comes to mind
are failed attempts
when her mouth was full

of someone else's tongue.

Bottled

She finds it in the woods
still smelling of spirits;

thick green glass
like Arctic ice, inside

the broken rigging
of a bird,

its wreck of bones.
She's sick with panic

feathers fluttering
in her throat,

her mouth too small
to sing it into flight.

The Voice

One day I found a voice
washed up on the beach —

a small colourless voice,
a piece of clear glass

scoured harmless by sand,
smooth as sea-handled stone.

I put it to my eye
but it didn't change the world

so I hurled it as far as I could.
It landed in deep grass

where it waits alone
to magnify the sun

to make fire.

Avocados

I like the way they fit the palm –
their plump Buddha weight,
the sly squeeze for ripeness,
the clean slit of the knife,
the soft suck
as you twist the halves apart,
the thick skin peeling easily.
Naked, they're slippery as soap.

I serve them for myself
sliced and fanned
on white bone china
glistening with olive oil,
or I fill the smooth hollow
with sharp vinaigrette
scooping out
the pale, buttery flesh.

Every diet you've ever read
strictly forbids them.

Bubbly

I want to go to your head tonight,
shake you up like a Grand Prix winner,
rocket to the ditzy stars,
set the moon's mirror-ball spinning,
lead you on a merry dance.
I want to fizz right past your brim
and keep on fizzing.
I want to get the wolf in you to whistle,
the world to wobble,
God to get the giggles.

Tonight I'm Marilyn
lying in this bath
of creamy magnolia.
I'm just dreamy,
blowing frothy kisses,
flirting in my foam bikini.
Can't you see
I want you in a lather?
Darling I'm your upper.
Pop me.

'I soothe your sore eyes'

I soothe your sore eyes
with my tongue,
explore their sockets,
slow as a snail
braving your brine.

I slide along
the ridge of bone,
circle your eyeball,
blind as a lychee
inside its skin,

a sea delicacy,
smooth as squid
hidden in its inky cave
feeling the gentle suck
of my tide.

Cambridge, 1948

They'd wished me a husband
but still, it's a *Prince's*
red salmon occasion.
Mum cuts off the crusts.
Dad cracks open a bottle.
Asti Spumanti.

My Big Day arrives.
I swan off
in a glossy black cab
waving a gloved hand.
Going away – years
rattling behind like tin cans.

I enter a fairytale city
white as a wedding cake –
the royal icing
of King's College Chapel.
My hand's on the knife
for a slice of it.

I'm not the second cousin
twice removed
whose name no one catches.
Nor the bridesmaid
in puppy fat and satin
missing the tossed bouquet.

Here Comes The Bride
in black cap and gown
giving nothing away.
On our first night
she smiles from the mirror.
I kiss her, whispering

I will.

Going My Way

I know everything is
when the midnight city clears

a wide and rain-shined street
as though for a queen's progress

and my car stretches like a cat
into a black limousine

purring without a change of gear
past darkened bars, the empty glass

shelters, angels in the cemetery
waving as I smile for the flash

of a speed camera
while in the street-lit trees

deceived birds sing for me
and there's no need to check the mirror

as with a click of my fingers
light after light after light

goes green...

Magpie

A crow –
but mobster-style –
shoe-shine black
spats white.
A flash character
dressed for dinner
on the hard shoulder.
Egg-filcher – the yolk
sliding easy down
your glossy throat.
You jab the hole
through the gold top,
suck the cream out.

A sharp eye
for glitter in the grass.
Dream-hoarder –
lining your nest
with silver foil,
bits of coloured glass,
diamanté, paste,
every single earring
I've ever lost.
You'd nick the ring
from my dead mum's finger,
the words right out
of our gaping mouths.

A loner at heart
I meet you
strutting in the road,
dipping your sticky
black beak.
You make me slow
down, almost stop –
a lazy hopping flap
at the last moment.
You eye me up
as I drive past.
Bad luck.
I salute you.

Other Halves

You. Pronoun. Plural. A second person
sleeping with his arm curled round your waist.
The full honey-moon to dip his fingers into.

Half a world away, I slip inside your empty house.
The door opens with a *sshhh* over white envelopes.
I move with rice-paper stealth through silent rooms

lifting dust from table tops, the arched backs of chairs.
The moon plays a light-fingered scale along the keys,
turns the vase on the mantelpiece into an urn.

Us. Framed in family photographs.
Side by side, hand in hand. Identical smiles
held a second too long to be natural.

Upstairs, drawers slide open smoothly on their runners.
You've taken the best. Left the bras with elastic
worming through the straps, the knickers edged in grey lace.

I make myself up. Your lips' contours glide over my own.
I bare my teeth for stains. Take a brush, the kind they use
for fingerprints, dust a soft blush along my cheekbones.

Here's your dress lying in a swoon of silk across the bed.
A shy rustle of tulle. Hooks and eyes. Sweetheart neckline.
Your boned bodice coddling my breasts.

The satin slippers pinch. I pirouette before the mirror
like the Swan Lake ballerina you kept inside
your jewellery box, bowing when you closed the lid.

Your presents loom, ghostly through the darkness.
Glossy paper crackles, a ribbon unravels,
sellotape peels slyly, skin from skin.

I open a canteen of cutlery – a thief's dream,
silver gleaming liquid in the moonlight
snug inside its velvet cushioned coffin.

Leaning closer, I glimpse your face, upside-down
and bloated in a spoon's polished bowl.
A sigh spirits it away.

Sharp tines glint. My mouth waters.
I weigh a knife's cool handle in my palm,
its balance ready to be tipped. Truth or Dare.

The blade points out into the night.
Under the white veil of a mosquito net
you wake to the taint of tarnish on your tongue.

Cold Blood

I am capable
of doing anything
for you –

take a wife,
young children,
your children.

I can make accidents –
wheels locking,
oncoming lights.

Quite painless.
Clean breaks.
Then while you're asleep

I will empty your house –
her dresses
in black plastic sacks,

toys to the needy,
photographs shoe-boxed
and buried.

I will feather the dust,
twirl away cobwebs
like candy-floss.

I will paint all the walls
amnesia white.
Nights, I will hover

over your heart
incubating
our future.

When you hatch from the dark
your eyelids will shutter
my face.

I will spirit you south
to a warm winter
next to the sea.

I will do
everything
for you –

feed you, teach you to speak,
your first word will be
my name.

Youngsters

We face each other
needy as blind fledglings,
obscenely greedy beaks
gawped wide,
stiff little tongues
screeching *ME!*
We could swallow one another.
No problem.
We weave our hate-nest tight,
cramp our puny wings.
Sharp quills break the skin.

At night, I teeter on the edge of dreams
shivering between the whistling sky
and the brutal concrete,
cowed by the squawk
of the fully-fledged world.
Failure, ugly, bald, plunges past.
I feel your beady eyes on me,
your eager beak
plucking up the guts
to peck
to push.

Wired

Since you left, everything I touch gives me a shock –
car doors, brass hand rails, even the cat
flicking her ears at my prickly stroke.

This dry spell sets my teeth on edge –
the sun fusing in its tin foil sky.
Hard water scurfs the kettle, scales the taps,

draws the skin across my cheekbones tight
as though I'm being scalped.
Stretching is a kind of Chinese burn.

I scratch my mock-croc shins until they bleed.
There's an itch in the middle
of my back that can't be reached.

The brush crackles through my hair
generating static – enough to light a bulb
above my head then blow the filament.

I'm like your cricket bat, warping in the attic
with its perished rubber grip,
its buckled wood needing linseed.

My nightdress sparks in the nylon darkness.
I'm waiting for oil rubbed warm between your palms,
for your hands to earth me.

Before/After

The surgeon's fingers
search my neck –
It's as large
as a small bird's egg
or flower bulb.
Growing.
A lump in my throat
that won't be swallowed

although I try,
stretching my neck
like a cartoon ostrich
with a whole orange
lodged in its oesophagus.
I watch it gliding
up and down –
my ripening Adam's apple.

X marks the spot
in indelible ink.
I gag in my pre-op sleep,
wake with my throat slit
and stitched back together.
A doll with the wrong head on.
Twist and my neck will split
like a juicy plum.

It heals keloid –
a line of gum
seeped from a cut tree,
the fresh gash of a bypass
through open country.
I test my new voice
bruised, husky.
I won't risk a shout.

I never leave the house
without a scarf.
After dark
I wear chokers.
When someone asks
I make a joke –
a mad lover
a cry for help.

I meet men
who'd try to suck me dry
like hot schoolboys
guzzling milk.
I let no one kiss it better.
I'll grow older,
let the years
wrinkle it away.

Although in dreams
I feel your tongue
still giving me the lie
sliding along
my scar's tight rope.
The night loosens,
slips its silk
from my bare shoulders.

Condemned

'Neither do I condemn thee: go, and sin no more.'
JOHN, 8. 11

Since then, I stay indoors
keep a slut's house – greasy plates,
wine sediment crusted in cups.
I let the fire go out.
I'm still smeared between the legs.
He won't speak – or if he does
my name's unleashed
from the sling of his voice.
The swineherd savours
the new wine of scorn
as he tips the swill out.
Trees hug their shadows tight.
Prostitutes cross the street.

The women thread bone needles of gossip.
At night they lay bad things at my doorstep
like a cat's cruel offerings –
a hare lip, a young boy's twisted foot,
an old woman's eyes like milky stones.
The lover, whose unexpected touch
once made my belly wince
clenches fists at me. I dream of us
behind the lattice screen – arid afternoons,
the shadows of carved leaves
filigreed across our skin. Something else
was dragged into the light that day.
The men are still afraid of it.

Passover. We prepare in ritual silence.
My husband slits the lamb's throat,
the one I nursed by hand,
talked to for hours in the fold.
He daubs blood on the gate-post.
Roast meat spits at me from the fire.
I knead the bread which will not rise,
crush the bitter herbs.

Tonight, I lie awake,
my spine curved from his
listening for the rush of wings
over the face of the earth,
the mothers wailing in the wilderness

and I wonder where *he* is
this night of our deliverance.
Has he left others like me
struggling to live with miracles –
like learning to walk again,
only painful this time, crippled,
with no one there to lift you from the dirt?
I heard the crowd parted for him like a sea,
spread torn palm leaves at his feet.
I would not hurl hosannas at his head.
Another dawn breaks red
like an unhealed wound. My eyes bloom
dark as bruises on the world.

Neighbours

I request the pleasure of your company.
No need to RSVP
just kick down the front door
splinter the safety chain.

Call me by my formal name. *Ms.*
You'll find milk clotting in the fridge.
Apples shrivelling in the bowl.
Help yourselves.

I'm the lady in waiting
screened behind the shower curtain,
snug as a heart
in a white enamel basin.

I've been listening to you
this past week –
the throb of bass through the floor,
the thump of next door's headboard,

the rasp of awkward keys,
the thwack of a perfect backhand
across a face.
I tell the time in theme tunes.

I'm ready to receive you now,
my hair spread out like weed
in the dark red water.
Be my guests.

The Glorious Dead

Summer sedates this city
with its formal squares and crescents,
its parades of shuttered white façades,
its gardens reserved for residents
guarded by ranks of black spears.

Pinned to his side I stroll
along the plinth-lined promenades,
between the well-drilled flower beds.
He points out features to admire.
The caryatids for instance –

lovely straight-backed girls,
models of deportment
balancing pillars on their heads.
He explains classical proportions.
I stare at their amputated arms.

Each morning I take the waters,
slipping into the witch's cauldron
of sulphurous steam. I watch
the crippled rich floating belly-up
marbled blue with veins like Stilton.

Then he takes me home to rest,
draws the heavy velvet curtains.
My eyeballs flicker behind shut lids.
A fly batters at the window.
Time slides and thickens like antique glass.

*

Standing on the balcony that day
in the rabid noon sun, the air
warped and rippled with heat.
I stared at the wrought iron tendrils
twisting like a single thought.

The sharp slam of a front door
sounded in the empty street
like the report of a funeral gun.
Bare feet flying
over blinding pavements.

They found her crouched
in the shadow of the bronze soldier,
damp forehead pressed against the stone,
tracing the fresh-cut letters of a name
with her naked finger.

*

Gilt-edged invitations. I circle
dazzling rooms, whispers rustling
like the stiff silk of my hobble skirt.
A word stirs a pearl drop earring.
Orchids wilt in black button-holes.

All evening he inflicts his gaze.
I feel it through my shoulder blades,
the aching of the bones like stumps
where a million years ago
I once had wings.

Letter Before Leaving

(Liverpool, 1944)

Fog-bound forever
the troop ship wallows
in its slick of filth.
Cooped in the hold we squabble
like red-wattled turkeys
on Christmas Eve.

On deck we rub our eyes
in disbelief of land.
All around the city rumbles
like a rumour of bombers
over the coast. Someone sighs
India...in a mist of breath.

Nothing exists
except this ghostly wharf,
the charcoal spar of the winch,
its dripping hook.
Children have given up
waving to us.

On look-out tonight
I heard a ship's horn calling
from the starless firth
like a lost dinosaur.
I could see your hand
in front of my face

like the night you had to walk
ahead of our car
searching for the road.
I crawled at funeral pace
following your torch
all the way home.

Nocturne

The future will be like this – alone
in the empty living room at dusk,
a sepia rose of damp blooming on the ceiling,
the garden hushed by steady rain –

wondering when it was that I gave up:
no conscious moment of decision,
just the piano gathering photographs and dust
before being sold. I never learnt

how to put both hands together,
although my skin remembers
the coldness of yellowed ivory
like touching your face goodbye.

I hold my breath for the final chord,
its soft-pedal andante.
You must have closed the door.
The silence leaves me

with something just beyond my reach –
like a word on the tip of my tongue,
or the octave stretch
of my too-small hand.

Bluebirds

In my sticky hands I held
summers with suns like toffees
in their own blue wrappers.
I'd lie in deep grass slowly chewing
the rationed sweetness,
aching my tongue, making it last.

I watched the swallows – bright bolts
of blue, forked like lightning or fish,
their white throats flashing past
quick as wishes. Only the sun
could catch their glossy wings
and make them glint.

Long afternoons of impossible loops,
wings carving the blue air
swooping on invisible dippers.
Even I knew, in my house noosed
by roads, when swallows flew high
it meant good weather.

And waking at the first chill,
the pillow like a mushroom, cool
against my cheek, the wires
blossomed briefly with birds
before the wind stripped them
and blew them south.

Victory

Winter '47 – the yards of bunting
and our Union Jack have been rolled up
and forgotten in the arctic attic.

Minus degrees for over a month.
Life becomes a subtraction –
colour and warmth taken away.

Snow falls day after day from skies
the tarnished silver of medals.
We huddle in our dug-out house.

Father is learning to write again,
filling old crosswords
with scrawled left-handed letters,

searching back editions of *The Times*
for answers to clues
he can't work out.

Mother's needles clack
while her tongue knits patterns
of monotonous gossip.

Long evenings I peer
at my Collins school atlas
silently reciting its litany of seas.

Too much reading
will damage your sight!
The coal splits with a sigh into flame.

At night my breath on the pane
mists like incense,
thawing a port-hole in frost.

Staring across the smothered fields
I try to trace the valley's lost road.
I fall asleep, listening

for the creak of snow giving way,
the buried pipes
that are waiting to burst.

Time Zones

He left de-mob Britain
greedy for life's full ration.
She remembers the docks –

little knots of families
waving white hankies
in frantic surrenders.

Thousands of streamers
trailing from the decks
tying ship to land.

She thought of Gulliver,
the shared bookshelf, black-out
and her brother's hand.

*

She hated phoning,
dragging the atlas down,
trying to find the hour
they shared awake.
The time difference.
The difference time makes.

His alien twang at Christmas,
summer in December,
turkey on the beach.
Words stuck in her throat.
The receiver clicked –
a snapped wishbone.

Instead they wrote –
long-distance stamps,
the blood-red petals
of an outback flower,
the Queen's head ageing
over forty years.

*

She leads him by the hand
through their home town.
He's forgotten the lingo
of its blitzed streets.
Façades survive like catch phrases –
Dig for Victory!, *We'll Meet Again.*

He puts the right names
to the wrong faces.
The split second
between their jokes
and his laughter
lasts decades.

*

New Year's Eve – photos, speeches, toasts

and streamers. He remembers the docks –
the tight knot of his father's grief
refusing to loosen into tears.

Slipping England's anchor with relief
he'd turned his back on the littered quay,
hadn't watched his little sister

waving till she disappeared.

*

She watches the thin, white trail across the sky
disperse. The newsreel flashes – 1952 –
the war-worn King waves his daughter goodbye.
Tired eyes, knowing she'll return a Queen.

Driving back, the wipers beat,
metronomes against the rain
timing the lonely waltz of satellites.
As she sleeps

his plane follows evening round the globe,
touching down at last
in the desert
in the middle of the night.

Legacy

My father had done well,
invested wisely.
He kept the front lawn clipped,
immaculate.

In the war
he put all the documents
he thought important –
his birth certificate,
the deeds to his house,
his last will and testament –
in a locked cash box
kept in the air-raid shelter.

But when a bomb caught him out
no one contested ownership
of the burnt bricks and mortar
and the two bits of paper
at either end of his life
seemed insufficient proof.
There wasn't much of him to bury.
He left me nothing.

But in the mirror
I have his thin hands
pushing the knot tight
on my Sunday tie.

Waltz of the Night Guard

A skyscraper sails
the city's slick of night

like a ghost ocean liner.
He is its captain

from the green-lit basement humming
like an abandoned engine room

to the rooftop in the stars
down through the gleaming lift shaft's

fifty empty floors.
He shuffles deserted offices

shackled with keys. Families
smile at him from noticeboards,

a message glides across a screen
Back soon... Back soon...

In the silent entrance hall
his footsteps echo marble,

a polished mahogany desk
curves like a ship's bar,

lilies still as moonlight
rest against the lip

of a tall glass vase
like girls waiting to be asked.

He shuts his eyes,
and risking a whistle in the dark,

slips his arm
around a waist of air.

The Survivor

My legs are sucked from their sockets
as thirty thousand tonnes of steel
slide beneath the water.

I watch him dragged backwards, haltered
by the oil-soaked life-belt
he hadn't had time to inflate.

There's a whinnying squeal in the darkness
and I'm trying to lead a blindfold horse
that rears in the burning stable,

though what wakes me now, lathered in sweat
these forty years later
is the silence.

Second Marriage

Today she is married again,
sitting silently in her wing-back chair
behind her veil of blindness.

I am a witness to this love –
her daughter kneeling beside her
opening the velvet box.

The ring replaces the one she lost;
its thinned gold slipped her finger
as easily as yesterday.

This one is smaller, tighter
and though she can't see the sun
catching its bright circle

she can feel it easing over her flesh,
the return of a familiar pressure,
her hand becoming her own again.

She twists it round and round
as my mother leans to kiss her,
and I wonder if she's remembering,

if not a time and place,
at least a sense of saying *yes*
to something, someone, once.

The Miracle Worker

(i.m. Elsie Evans, 1906-2001)

She performed them quietly,
the touch of her hands
stilling my storm.

Lame, she could run
through the walls between years
into her father's arms again.

Deaf, she could hear him
talking to her in the night,
finding the right words this time.

Blind, she recognised strangers,
christening them
her own flesh and blood.

I became legion –
her mother, her daughter,
sometimes even myself

and though she was mute,
she told me my future
in the runes of her face.

I left her falling asleep,
her eyes closing slowly
over my ghost.

Tonight she leaves me awake,
walking on the dark water,
raising my dead.

Cremation

Today I am burning my family
because I love them,
because I want to see their eyes
blazing fiercely again,
to feel their warmth on my skin
like a touch.

Today I am burning my family
because they are mine,
because I remember their names,
know the backs of their hands,
because when I stare at their faces
I hear voices and laughter,
because I know the before and after
and where that new car is going.

Today I am burning my family
because they trust in the future too much,
their faces shining like stars,
and I know the rocks they are steering towards;
divorces and cancer,
or the slow exposure of age,
each day a photograph taken
simply to use up the film.

Today I am burning my family,
but this is no war or holocaust;
look they are smiling as they're released,
moths of ash fluttering into the dusk,
a rope of white smoke they are climbing up,
disappearing into an empty sky.

Miserere

You are lining up your normal pills –
a small white one with a long name,
a slick capsule of pink and black.
Your pulse slows. Rain.
Dusk slurring into night.
By nine, you're dead to the world.

In another life, you took me once
to hear Allegri's masterpiece.
We huddled in the stone cold, awed,
as the highest note a choirboy can reach
soared free of the bars of manuscript
and hung in the twilight of the church.

3 a.m. The rain's still lashing.
You've left my side,
stumbled in the darkness
down the stairs. I find you,
naked and bleeding, moaning *fuck it*
in a broken voice.

The Architect

You drew dream houses –
the kind that bankrupted noble families
four centuries ago – gothic follies
glimpsed through mist by moonlight,
towers and cupolas enclosed
by the darkness of midsummer oaks,
windows with diamonds of glass,
tall barley-twist chimneys
and a ghost of smoke.

All sketched tremulously
as though your pencil point
picked up minute vibrations
from an earthquake of the past.
Moth delicate –
the warmth of a fingertip
could have smudged their tracery,
left skin glittering
with graphite dust.

Out driving
you'd suddenly stop the car
in some lonely place
of moor or mountain.
I'd watch you walk away from me,
framing the landscape
with your hands, in love
with what wasn't there,
never would be.

Out of Season

This is all we could afford –
a one-star room
with a dribbling shower,
grey towels,
a thin tablet of soap.

You scrape a chair
across the mock-marble floor.
I hang my flimsy dresses
from thin wire shoulders.
The empty suitcase sags.

At breakfast, we stick to hard facts –
the average rainfall in January,
the local flora and fauna.
The table's littered
with shattered bread rolls.

Outside, the wind piles clouds
like dirty underwear.
We pose alone in front
of scaffolded monuments
for photos we won't develop.

Days spent in silent museums
learning the island's bloody past.
Bored waiters serve us dinners
of tough, char-grilled steaks.
We leave cold smiles

of fat on our plates.
The night air pimples
my bare arms. Cabs with plastic
dashboard Madonnas
keep bringing us back

to this bed with its hard
bolster pillow, its sheets
of old paperback yellow,
the crawling caterpillars
of green candlewick.

Lips sealed, we slip
into its tight envelope.
The crab of your hand
inches towards me, shrinking
my nipple to a hard knot.

Sex judders through us
like rubber wiper blades across dry glass.
We cling to the edges in the dark
listening to the slow hand-clap
of a shutter in the wind.

The Wilderness Years

The devil gave me these wings –
feathers plucked from the breasts of doves
then bosticked onto cardboard cut-outs,
a contraption of straps to keep them in place,
all topped off with a halo of tinsel.

It was enough to convince you
as you pirouetted barefoot, tiptoe
at the pinnacle of a dreaming spire.
Weather-vain, your future was mapped out below you –
a kingdom of bright green manicured quads.

From that distance I must have looked like a vision
because when Satan whispered something about God
you dizzied and jumped, your shadow a hand
between me and the sun as I broke
your fall and proved us both human.

We came to at night – the crowd had long gone,
blood and feathers in the gutter like a road kill,
and you draped in my arms, a pietà.
We are frozen in that attitude still – your spirit
unrisen, my wings invisible and heavy as stone.

Deciding not to leave you

after all, reminds me once again of Prince,
the collie next door to our first house.
Leashed for days in the grey-slated yard.
He offered a paw through the bars of the gate.
Gently, he licked my face and neck.

I saw him return from short, choke-chained walks.
In summer he lay flat out in the dirt,
his belly a bath mat's discoloured cream,
worn patches of skin at his elbows,
dreams twitching his feet, baring his teeth.

In winter, he cringed in the whip of the rain,
ears flat to his skull, the old rope of his tail
tucked between shivering legs. He made his bed
by trampling ferns in imaginary woods.
Tonight I'll lie on the side which hurts less.

Slash

Next day it burns like acid
her piss squeezed drop by drop
as if from a pipette
and red as Beaujolais.

She gulps down pints of water
like she's dying of thirst,
tries to flush him out
of her infected system.

But the stinging persists,
a reminder (as if she needed one)
like the knot tied
in the condom by the bed.

Each time she tells herself
will be the last, each time
she's lost for words
as he performs his miracle –

getting blood out of a stone.

Going There Again

She used to live here once –
this room at the end
of the world's longest corridor.

Behind these double doors
she'd sit listening for his footsteps,
stiffening like an ivory queen

while swans shifted feathers in their sleep
out on the ice-locked river.
Cloistered by winter, she waited.

I sense her on the other side
still tensed for the lifted fist,
and I turn and run

back down the echoing length of my life,
hurling my weight against
heavy-hinged doors –

year after year
closing slowly behind me
like astonished mouths.

Solo

She takes nothing with her
but the crows' feet
round her eyes,
the white ring of skin
on her naked finger.

All down the long avenue of pines
her headlights lift
each tree into place
like the ripple of arms
in a *corps de ballet*

as the swan passes.

Hints for Outback Motoring

The guide book lists *Essentials for the Trip*:
detailed maps
tool set
repair kit
fan belt
fuel can (full)
funnel
jump leads
spark plugs
pump
radiator hose
two spare tyres
fire extinguisher
tow rope
black tape
pressure gauge
axe and spade
water.

In the event of a breakdown which isn't due
to a snapped fan belt
burnt out spark plug
split radiator hose
flat tyre (or two)
or electrical fire,
stay with your vehicle.
Someone will find you.

To pass the time in a remote area
try to remember everything
your father ever told you
about the internal combustion engine.
Once you think you know
what the distributor is for
start sipping the water.

When it gets dark
there will be more stars
than you've ever seen before.
Try to remember
the names of constellations
you once knew by heart.
Recite yourself to sleep
on a groundsheet of detailed maps.
Someone will find you.

Next morning
you need to decide,
once and for all,
your Desert Island Discs.
Sing them silently
whilst sipping water
even more slowly
than the day before.

By noon you'll be playing loony tunes
with spanners from your tool kit
on the hot bonnet
of your stayed-with vehicle.
Use the radiator hose
to improvise a didgeridoo.
Sun arise.
Someone will find you.

Make large paper planes
out of the detailed maps.
Black insulation tape torn into strips
can be used to remove unwanted hair.
The Bible. The Complete Works of Shakespeare.
Take a sniff of fuel from the fuel can (full).

Soon the flying doctors will be looping the loop
skywriting your name.
If you could only remember
the author of your favourite book.
At this point you might
want to take an axe
to the mirage of a tree
then gauge your pressure.

By mid-afternoon
the only luxuries in the world
are shade and water
and nothing looks useful
except the tow rope and spade.
Practise tying slip knots, then start digging
whilst taking the odd nip
of petrol to keep going.

Night again.
Wander into the desert
clutching a detailed map.
When you think you've reached
The Middle of Nowhere
sprinkle the last drops of water
over your head
while trying to remember
your name.

Pour petrol letters
into the sand.
Watch HELP burn
and then die down.
Wrap the black tape around your eyes
then lift your face
to the smoke-veiled stars.
Stay where you are.
Someone will find you.

Industrial Light and Magic

Where does Obi Wan go?
He stares down at his son who won't take
I don't know for an answer.

So he improvises, tearing up
a scrap of paper until he holds
a snowstorm in his fist.

When the body dies
the spirit is released —
like this!

And the boy laughs
at the sudden blizzard
spinning round his head.

But he knows its just a trick,
like Father Christmas, or the man
with doves and laughter up his sleeve.

So when the drift has settled,
he asks again, insists
but where does he GO?

On the frozen screen
the light sabre flickers
as it strikes the empty cloak.

He stares down at his son
the pale sheet of his face
lifted to him, and he feels

the glass world shaken,
all his answers flying up
into the dark empire.

The Code-breaker

He stayed up late all winter
to crack the code of birdsong, slowing
their voices down, transcribing
note by note the blackbird's
enigma variations.

He meditated to the mantra
of the cuckoo and the dove,
searched for a solution
to the complex equations
set by the nightingale.

He never found an answer,
until the night he left the house
with his recorder and a knife,
returning hours later,
the blade stuck with white feathers.

They found him stiff with listening,
but when they played it back
there was only the hiss of silence
then something like a sob
just before the tape ran out.

The Legend of Apollo

They wished for the moon
then granted it themselves
appearing in its silence
like clumsy angels
dressed in white
with haloes of vapour.

They learnt to walk again
through the dream dust
of long dead seas,
to gaze like children
at their blue-glass sphere
tissued in mist.

They returned home as gods
with a cargo of rocks
leaving only relics
of their miracle –
a flag of stars,
footprints that have lasted

an eternity,
and this photograph,
its bleed of colour
in the night's negative –
a nuclear family
smiling at the dark.

NOTE: Charles Duke, one of the Apollo astronauts,
left a snapshot of his family on the moon.

Love in the Republic

The couples wait their turn,
women twisting rings round
swollen fingers, their throats
hung with silver crosses.
The men's shirts stain between
their shoulder blades. Salt stings
the tips of tongues licking
the seams of thin roll-ups.
Smoke curls from silent lips.

El patrón inspects the line
palming grimy dollars.
The shack is sun-baked brick.
Inside – a soiled mattress,
naked bulb, frayed wires.
A stifled moan disturbs
the heat. A lizard flickers
from a fading slogan.
The queue shuffles forward.

The Cricket Test
(for Norman Tebbit)

This ball looks soaked
in week-old blood,
its stitched seam of skin
reminds me of things,

and this wooden club
with its good grip –
I've seen something like it
shatter a life.

These staves with sharpened ends –
are eyes dangerous here too?
This studded boot
could tread a red tattoo.

I know this helmet –
the grin behind
the metal grille
as the gun butt is lifted.

Except I don't understand
why the uniform is white –
you can see where a man
has wiped his hands

and this blood rose sewn
into the chest, I'm sorry
I can't tell what it means
but I know English well:

leg break – a favourite punishment
square cut, *hook* – both close your eyes
stump – a present from a bomb
boundary – what you get shot crossing.

You say this is only a game.
Where I'm from they play it
deadly serious. Please,
will you let me pass now?

Christenings

Upstream a forest
of flesh has been felled,
a log-jam of bodies

spun in the swift current,
caught in the teeth
of foaming rapids

until the river widens and slows,
draining its delta of veins
into the sea.

By day the women keep
to the shallows, pounding
their white sheets pink.

By night they come down
to the river's cold cradle
to drink its communion.

They wade deep into darkness.
As each son drifts past
they turn his bruised face

gently towards them,
kiss the eyes closed,
give him a name.

Relics
(for Kelvyn)

The causeway is a fine thread
tying the island to the mainland shore,
a fragile mooring cut twice a day by tides.
It feels like an act of faith as we set foot
on this narrow parting of the North Sea.

Holy Island. Seagulls' sanctuary.
The endless keening of the birds.
Life lived close-cropped like turf.
Monks kneel in our minds stiff as stone
with worship, intoning salt prayers.

Battling along the beach, heads bent,
past the stranded hulls of upturned boats,
we fight to breathe like fish,
hooked and flapping,
slapped dead on the wet decks.

The ruined priory still does penance,
wind-whipped, strafed by sand, roofless
except for one communicating arch
whittled thin as bone, which leaps
the gulf between two pillars.

A small victory as you light a cigarette,
cupping your hands to protect the tiny flame.
Your voice takes shelter in my name
as you slip your hand to share my pocket's warmth.
The sun sets in a streak of gold leaf

lending sandstone a brief radiance.
We exchange gritted kisses in the failing light,
then turn to beat the tide back home.
Behind us the Rainbow Arch is inked against the sky
braced to carry the weight of one more night.

Sand

That last spring I seemed to guess.
In one long dusk I harvested the garden,
hung clusters of flowers from the rafters.
I pressed violets between the leaves
of dictionaries and bibles, filled
whole seed trays with keep-sake petals.

The summer burned hotter, turning
the hydrangea heads coppery,
rosebuds into bunches of dried blood.
Their dusty pot pourri still lingers.
I fall asleep, my fingers tracing
the wallpaper's trellis of honeysuckle.

I am the last one left in this valley,
empty and brown as a beggar bowl.
All day I sweep the desert from my steps.
The slate floors crunch like emery boards.
Wood loses its lustre, dulls to the matt
of a cataract eye. My skin cracks like a lizard's.

I turn on taps out of habit.
The plumbing is racked by shuddering sobs.
I risk bad luck – umbrellas blooming indoors
like black silk poppies. I've spent hours
sifting the attic for grass-stained tennis balls,
shutting my eyes, inhaling the past.

No twilight. Night falls like a blade.
In my dry bed, I dream rain;
fat droplets on waxy laurel leaves,
clouds the colour of tear-run ink,
the subtleties of mist. I dive into a pool
and wake. The dunes curve their scimitars.

Silence – except for the tinnitus
inside my head, its constant shush and whisper.
The horizon shifts in the moonlight,
a drift surges, snapping a telegraph pole
like a pencil, a forest of pines
shrinking to Christmas trees.

I think of the pale green domes of cathedrals
buried out there like unhatched eggs.
Soon this house will go blind, its windows silted,
the sun eclipsed, an hour glass twist
in the fireplace. I already sense its silkiness,
the kiss that will stopper my mouth.